CW00420239

1

Copenhagen Travel Guide

The Top 10 Highlights in Copenhagen

Table of Contents

Introduction

It's for good reason that Copenhagen always rates highly on those coveted "Best in the World" cities lists for environmental friendliness, livability and other desirable modern city traits. Copenhagen is one of those cities that just works. Packed with impressive castles and palaces, dotted with gardens and picturesque waterways, countless reasons abound for paying a visit to the Danish capital.

Of all the gems to visit in Copenhagen, Rosenborg Slot is by far the greatest favorite among tourists. Upon setting foot inside the Rosenborg, visitors cannot help but feel like they have entered a gigantic royal dollhouse, as the castle houses a splendid collection of royal artifacts in well maintained rooms. Fans of real life fairy tale majesty will be impressed by the Mirror Room and displays of Royal China.

Frederiksborg Slot is an impressive castle that houses Denmark's Museum of National History. Roam the magnificent castle halls and admire the vast artwork collection. Do not miss out on the Baroque-style Royal Gardens that offer some of the best castle views on the far side of the lake.

Another magnificent castle, Amalienborg Slot boasts exquisite Rococo buildings and is the winter home of the

Danish Royal Family. There is also free daily entertainment here in the form of the Changing of the Royal Guard which takes place at noon.

A visit to Copenhagen is not complete without a tour of Christianshavn, one of the most highly sought after neighborhoods in the city. This fashionable, diverse and lively part of Copenhagen cannot be missed for its distinctive personality and attractions that offer an abundance of entertainment venues to enjoy.

One of the main highlights of Copenhagen is Christiania, a self-proclaimed autonomous neighborhood within Christianshavn. Home to around 1000 permanent residents and notorious for its legal cannabis trade, Christiania is a must-visit on any Copenhagen itinerary, primarily for its alternative way of life.

At the National Gallery of Denmark, art lovers can enjoy some of the best artwork of the Western hemisphere. Old meets new in this unique museum of funky interactive exhibits. To learn even more about Danish culture, visit the Nationalmuseet. Housed in a Victorian mansion, the national museum provides an intriguing history of Denmark from the prehistoric era to the present day.

One of Europe's best known tourist attractions, Tivoli was established during a period when pleasure gardens were all the rage. Copenhagen's version is particularly lovely, offering an ideal spot to admire gorgeous blooms, as well as a creative outlet and social center for performing troupes. Visitors can enjoy the many amusement rides, games, restaurants, shops and seasonal festivals.

To many, Nyhavn defines what Copenhagen is all about. Take a stroll along the quay of the old harbor and take in the special atmosphere of the old port. You could even have some of the famous Nyhavn ice cream or beer and listen to live music bands play outside.

Beyond the traditional must-sees, Copenhagen has a lot to offer. Easily the perfect city break destination, Copenhagen is easy to walk, bike-friendly and packed with historic buildings, sparkling canals, green spaces and delicious cuisine. Foodies will adore Copenhagen, as will lovers of art and design. In the capital of the maritime nation of Denmark, many great tourist attractions await you.

1. Frederiksborg Slot

Frederiksborg Slot is the largest Renaissance-era building in the whole of Scandinavia. The Danish castle is nestled on three islands next to the Hillerod castle lake, north of Copenhagen. Surrounded by exotic sweet scented gardens, the castle makes for a wonderful addition to every traveler's historical experience in Denmark, and for one of the best day trips from Copenhagen.

Around the 17th century, during the early decades at the start of the Renaissance period, King Christian IV had the Frederiksborg Slot built. The castle soon became one of the grandest structures of Renaissance craftsmanship and authentic architecture. It today remains the epitome of Danish style design and historical significance.

The castle's medieval gardens and ancient portrait collection make up the most scenic displays for tourists. Visitors can have a peek at the significant collection of portraits, modern art and exotic illustrations, including the famous painting of Queen Caroline Mathilde.

The castle's Neptune Fountain was commissioned for the middle courtyard and remains a symbol of Denmark's superior position as a leading Baltic power of the 1600s. This is one of the castles most awe-inspiring and splendid exhibits.

Visitors should walk past Mint Gate, through Mint Bridge then step inside the lavish bed of exotic flowers resting within the Baroque-style Palace Garden. The Palace Garden originated as a romantic setting for King Frederik I's Bath House Palace, which is still occasionally used by the Danish royal family.

Complete with parterre flower beds and symmetrical alignment, the festive cascades and royal monograms are sure to catch your attention during the garden tour. Visitors can also explore the insides of stable wings at the castle, or take a tour through the round towers that were built in 1562 on the southern end of the island.

On your way inside the castle, you will be led past the historical pavements of the Museum of National History which has resided within the castle walls since 1878. At the Museum, visitors can browse the photo archive and purchase some memorable images.

The museum depicts Denmark's history through a rich collection of historical paintings, portraits, decorative arts and furniture. A tour of the museum will bring you into the lives of people and events that have helped shape Danish history from the Middle Ages to the 21st century. This tour will enable you to learn about 500 years of Danish history.

The museum's historical interiors, coupled with the castle's splendid rooms offer a sensuous impression of the changing epochs and styles, along with the social conventions of the times. The portrait collection found here is the largest and most significant in Denmark, with new works being added to the collection continually.

2. Rosenborg Slot

One of Scandinavia's most famous kings, Christian IV built Rosenborg Slot in the early 17th century. Rosenborg is a royal castle that features 400 years of splendor, including the Crown Jewels, Royal Regalia, and other royal art treasures.

Among the main highlights of the castle is the Knights' Hall with its coronation thrones and three life-size silver lions that stand guard. Tapestries hang on the walls in commemoration of historic battles between Denmark and Sweden.

The well preserved interiors will take you on a journey in time where you can experience the king's private writing cabinet, bathroom and peek at wax figures of former royals. The castle also houses an exquisite collection of Flora Danica, and one of the finest Venetian glass collections in the world.

The crowns of Danish kings and queens embellished with table-cut stones, gold and enamel ornamentation are held in special vaults. The crown jewels consist primarily of 4 garnitures: a diamond set, a pearl set, a ruby set and an emerald set – the emeralds being among the finest in the world.

Also view the portraits of Queen Caroline Mathilde and Johan Friedrich Struensee, dated from 1824 and 1771 respectively. Caroline Mathilde was married to King Christian VII but had a love affair with Struensee, the king's physician. Struensee led the country for almost 2 years when the king was too ill to govern, but was arrested and executed in 1772, while Caroline Mathilde was exiled to Germany.

Be sure to complete your tour of Rosenborg slot by visiting its sister museum at Amalienborg Palace where you can view a grand display of royal history from the mid-19th century to the present day.

3. Amalienborg Slot

Regarded as one of the most outstanding works of Danish Rococo architecture, Amalienborg Slot was constructed in the 1700s, and comprises four identical buildings within the castle square: Christian VII's Palace, Frederik VIII's Palace, Christian VIII's Palace and Christian IX's Palace.

One of the main palace attractions is the Museum which is situated within Christian VIII's palace. Here visitors get to experience the royal life, past and present through the private interiors of the most recent kings and queens, as well as an exhibit on the monarchy today and its numerous traditions.

The museum's scope stretches back 150 years to Christian IX and Queen Louise, who were known as the "in-laws of Europe" as four of their children ascended to the thrones of Denmark, England, Russia and Greece. The rooms of the royals remain intact to this day, each reflecting the modern taste of its period, as well as the personalities of the monarchs, be it in the military, knightly or Victorian style.

On Saturdays, visitors are granted admittance into the royal reception rooms on the piano mobile, which are still used by the royal family. A large garden also offers insight into 21st century royal life and the monarchy.

Amalienborg is also known for the changing of the Royal Guard known in Danish as Den Kongelige Livgarde. Every day, the guard marches from their barracks through the streets past Rosenborg Slot to arrive at Amalienborg Slot at noon.

On special occasions such as the birthday of the queen on 16th April, the Royal Guard will wear red guard gala and hold gala flags with the royal coat of arms displayed. Both the Lieutenant Watch and the King's Watch of the Royal Guard are accompanied by the tambour corps and music.

4. Christiansborg Slot

Situated on the small island of Slotsholmen, Christiansborg Slot is one of Copenhagen's most iconic landmarks. With a history dating more than 800 years, the Baroque-style palace was for a long time the principal residence of the Danish royal family. Although the royal family now resides in Amalienborg Slot, Christiansborg remains at the center of Danish rule.

The castle houses the Danish Parliament, the Ministry of State and the Supreme Court, in addition to several Royal Reception Rooms. Parts of this royal palace are used by the royal family to hold a variety of events and functions, while the Oval Throne Room gives way to the balcony on which Danish monarchs are proclaimed.

The Great Hall is the most imposing room in the palace, for this is where the Queen's tapestries are housed. In 1990, to mark the occasion of Her Majesty Queen Margrethe II's fiftieth birthday, the Danish business community ordered a gift of eleven tapestries in a spectacular series that depicts 1000 years of Danish history.

5. Christianshavn

Situated just across the Knippels Bro Bridge, Christianshavn is officially a part of Copenhagen's city center and a much desired neighborhood for Copenhageners to reside in. This is primarily due to its central location, its unique maritime atmosphere and the many bars and restaurants it houses.

Christianshavn is home to narrow cobbled streets and cozy canal-side cafes where visitors can sit and enjoy a cold beer. There are also Michelin-starred restaurants for the luxury traveler, such as the world-famous *noma*, a gourmet restaurant which has four times been ranked the "Best Restaurant in the World" by British Restaurant Magazine.

noma is a popular dining spot in Copenhagen situated in a renovated harbor-front warehouse in a setting that adds to its appeal. *noma*'s Chef Rene Redzepi excels in Scandinavian cuisine and offers exceptionally good food. Foodies must book in advance for your world-class gastronomic experience as there is often a couple of months wait before you can get a table here.

Another Christianshavn highlight is the Danish Architecture Center (DAC), which is the main exhibition space for architecture in Denmark. DAC is the ideal starting point for those who wish to learn more about world-famous Danish architecture and city planning.

Visitors here can experience a broad spectrum of exhibitions that typically have an overarching theme or a special focus on a Danish or international architect. The exhibitions seek to communicate the meaning of architecture in an engaging and interactive way that sometimes also makes active use of the surrounding city space.

DAC also holds architecture tours of Copenhagen during the summer months. During this time you may join a Sunday afternoon walk in English that will have you exploring both the old and new parts of the city. If you prefer to explore the city on your own, DAC offers podruns and podwalks on their site that will guide you on a running or walking tour, while telling you about the architecture as you pass it by.

In addition to the exhibitions, DAC hosts a variety of activities, debates, workshops and guided tours that constantly generate new ideas and inspirations.

The DAC shop holds the largest collection of books on architecture and city planning in Denmark. This is a good place to shop for a gift or souvenir featuring a fine assortment of Danish design. If you get hungry, take a break at the café and indulge in its popular lunch and brunch menu to be enjoyed with an excellent view of the city and harbor.

Visitors to Christianshavn can also admire the décor and enjoy an extraordinary performance at The Royal Danish Opera. The Royal Danish Opera House totals 41,000 square meters with five of its fourteen storeys being subterranean. Decorated in southern German Jura Gelb limestone with the foyer featuring a Sicilian Perlatino marble, the main opera stage can seat an audience of 1400.

The Opera House auditorium wall which faces the foyer is covered in maple wood, while the ceiling of the main auditorium has been adorned with 24 carat gold leaf sheets. The interior décor of the Royal Danish Opera features bronze reliefs and light sculptures among others.

Nordatlantens Brygge or North Atlantic House is an art center at which visitors can experience North Atlantic culture, research and business. It is here that people from Denmark, the north Atlantic and the rest of the world meet and inspire one another.

The house features exhibitions rooms and holds events including music, dances, films, lectures and performances to give a taste of North Atlantic art and culture in the setting of an old 16th century warehouse.

For more than 200 years, the building served as the center for shipping traffic between the North Atlantic and Denmark. Today, the historic warehouse is a thriving cultural centre dedicated to the art and culture of Denmark's former North Atlantic colonies of Iceland, Greenland and the Faroe Islands.

Because artists from the North Atlantic are frequently inspired by the light, nature and landscapes of their region, this lends a fiercely, bodily, visual and musical quality to their art. As such, the rustic, maritime spirit of the old warehouse with its exposed rafter ceilings and raw plank floors offers a beautiful and unique contrast to the artworks on display.

Be sure to visit the cultural center for a first hand impression of this intriguing harbor front location. There is also a splendid café on site at which you can rest your tired feet. The warehouse is also home to *noma*, the Michelin-starred restaurant and a temple to Nordic cuisine.

Situated on Papiroen Island, Copenhagen Street Food is the Danish capital's first and only genuine street food market. Here you will find small food trucks stocking delicious sustainable street food from all corners of the globe. You can enjoy your food indoors in the raw halls or in the sun overlooking the waterfront.

The street food market is at once very Copenhagen-like as it is foreign. Scents of Mexican, Korean, Italian and Danish food float from the small colorful food trucks. The great raw halls in maritime settings offer cheap street food, in addition to culture and sustainability. Coffee, beer and other drinks are also available.

While some food trucks offer organic food, the priority is that the food tastes good, was made from scratch and is sustainable in that ingredients are local produce, as opposed to having been transported over long distances. The motto here is "genuine, honest and aesthetic", and while some dishes may cost more, there is always at least one option going for DKK 50 or that price range.

Copenhagen Street Food is also a haven for creative souls such as musicians and artists, as there are often events and activities going on in between meals. Relax in deck chairs out on the pier when the sun is out and enjoy one of the best city views as you munch on delicious food. Because Copenhagen Street Food operates in accordance with the weather, it may open later or close earlier if it rains a lot.

Our Savior is one of the most famous churches in Denmark, made even more so by its famous Spire. Inaugurated in 1752, the serpentine spire has made for a popular pastime among Danes who climb its 400 steps to the top where Our Savior himself stands atop a golden globe to keep watch over the royal city of Copenhagen.

From 90 meters above street level, and with the last 150 steps on the outside of the spire, the view from the spire's top has previously been voted the best in the city by

Copenhageners. Rundertaarn is yet another popular site that offers some of the best views of city.

Experimentarium is a science centre at which you are able to touch, see and experience science in all its forms. With a great waterfront view of Nyhavn and the Royal Danish Opera, visitors can experiment and learn about themselves, their body and senses.

Through play and exciting experiences, you can learn about the world as you ride a reverse steering bike, try to control your brainwaves, guess smells, test your reaction time and energy spent on the rowing machine or roar louder than a lion. There are plenty of activities at the Experimentarium to allow for hours of exploration.

Refshaleoen Island comprises an old industrial area that was once home to one of the largest shipyards in the world. Today, the island houses creative office spaces, music festivals, activity centers and restaurants. Situated a mere 15 minute bike ride from the city center, the island takes the shape of a peaceful oasis in the middle of a bustling Copenhagen.

An old historic landmark gone trendy, the island is today the venue for many fun and interesting sporting activities.

At the Urban Ranger Camp, visitors can experience the rush of walking on ladders and ropes at a height of 50 meters. Adventurous travelers will enjoy challenging themselves both physically and mentally at this camp. The camp is the highest of its kind in the world and makes for an exhilarating playground for challenging fun, right up under the roof of the old shipyard's giant halls.

Also located on Refshaleoen island is the Paintball Arena. Copenhagen's Paintball Arena is Europe's largest indoor paintball and activity center. In addition to paintball, visitors can enjoy lazertag, human football, bungee running, in addition to many other multisport events. Visitors must reserve to play in advance so be sure to call or email ahead.

The Blocs & Walls Climbing Center on Refshaleoen island is the largest of its kind in Scandinavia. In addition to the state-of-the-art climbing walls and boulders, the center boasts brand new facilities, a cafeteria and training center.

6. Christiania

Also located within Christianshavn is the "Freetown" of Christiania. Christiania was founded in 1971 by a group of hippies who cut a hole in the fence to the military barracks in Badmandsgade. The Danes then occupied an abandoned military barracks on this site and proceeded to develop their own set of societal rules, which were completely independent of the government of Denmark.

Soon after its founding, the area became known as "Pusher Street", where visitors could buy pot and hash, but no hard drugs, from the various stalls. Many of Christiania's original settlers continue to live in the collectively controlled village that has a clear 70s hippie feel to it. The green car-free neighborhood is today best known for the different way of life of its autonomous inhabitants.

Roughly 1000 people live in Christiania today, with most of them having built their homes by themselves, which gives the area a very interesting architectural feel. Freetown Christiania comprises a diversity of eco-restaurants, art galleries, workshops, music venues, cheap organic eateries and beautiful nature that offer all sorts of cultural experiences.

The area is open to the public and local Christianites give guided tours. This is a great way to experience the special Christiania vibe as the guides have lived there most their lives. At the entrance there are signs indicating the dos and don'ts of the area. Be sure to follow the rules to ensure a pleasant tour of Christiania.

Grey Hall is the largest concert hall in Christiania which was originally built in 1891 as a riding venue for the army barracks. Upon the founding of Christiania, the hall became the focal point for everything art and music related. Since then, many local and international performers have had shows here.

Christmas in Christiania is also celebrated in the Grey Hall beginning with a bazaar and large market. The venue also hosts Christmas Eve celebration events.

Christiania's Gay House is the cultural meeting spot for gay, lesbian and trans-gendered individuals in Copenhagen. The venue hosts cultural projects, music and theatre performances, exhibitions, parties and speaker events.

Located in the idyllic Bossehave, Gay House or Bossehuset in Danish is a membership based organization with an administration committee responsible for the economy and maintenance of the house. House activities are governed by a weekly meeting that is open to all.

Housed inside an old army hall, Loppen is an alternative concert venue that has hosted music concerts since 1973.

The bare and rustic interiors of the building are also home to a flea market, art gallery and restaurant.

Loppen is a collective organization with no head person in charge. All decisions about the venue and what concerts to showcase are made unanimously during weekly meetings. The work done at Loppen is all voluntary and designed to contribute in keeping the bar prices as low as possible.

Christiania Smedie is the oldest business in Christiania. Although its blacksmiths originally produced furnaces, during the seventies they shifted focus to supplying transportation for the car-free community. The first crate bike featuring a spacious crate at the front was launched in the 1980s.

Christiania is also home to Morgenstedet, an organic, vegetarian eatery that has existed for more than 20 years under the concept of collectivism and voluntary workforce. The café is housed in a small white washed building with a pebbled front yard that's ideal for lounging in the sun. The interior features quirky furniture and an open countryside kitchen with an antique stove.

Visitors can sample the homemade vegetarian fare, based on organic ingredients, choosing between two hot dishes and several salads.

While your food will be brought to your table, you are expected to pick your water and cutlery from a self-service table, and clear your own table once done. This is part of the Morgenstedet philosophy that guests should contribute to the maintenance of the café and hence keep the prices low.

For 40 years, Christiania existed under special conditions, with constant clashes and conflicts between the Christianites and the Danish state. After many years of uncertainty about Christiania's future, an agreement was entered and the Foundation Freetown Christiania established in 2012. The foundation today co-owns Christiania with the Danish state.

7. Nationalmuseet

Nationalmuseet is Denmark's National Museum, which houses exhibitions from the periods of the Stone Age, Viking Age, the Renaissance, the Middle Ages, as well as Modern Danish History.

Situated within The Prince's Palace, the museum's gallery comprises a wide corridor with displays of exquisite handicrafts. The ceiling's stucco, the floors of oak parquet and the panels are all believed to be original, while the stove and furniture date from the early 1700s.

The museum is Denmark's largest and most important historical and cultural museum which hosts a wide variety of fascinating exhibitions. You can easily spend an afternoon in the various exhibitions, and a whole day can also fly by as there is just so much to see here.

The museum also features an extensive ethnographical collection, in addition to a collection of near eastern and classical antiquities, a toy museum, and a medal and coin collection. Visitors can also tour Klunkehjemmet, a Victorian apartment that has practically remained unchanged since the year 1890.

The museum is a time-machine with its collections on Egyptian mummies, the Vikings, and even a hash stall from Christiania. Some of the most famous historical finds from ancient times are housed in the museum, which make for extraordinary and exciting exhibits.

The Danish Antiquity features prominent national treasures like the over 3000 years old Sun Chariot, the Egtved Girl from the Bronze Age, as well as an extraordinary collection of Viking Age archaeological finds. Another intriguing find is the Huldremose Woman with her well-preserved remains which are estimated to date from the 1st decade of the 1st century AD.

8. Statens Museum for Kunst

The National Gallery of Denmark is a showcase of outstanding collections of Danish and international art dating back to the previous seven centuries. Also known as Statens Museum for Kunst, the National Gallery is Denmark's largest art museum which features regular temporary exhibitions, in addition to its excellent permanent collection.

The museum also houses the Danish National Art Library, which is open to anyone with a keen interest in architecture and the visual arts. Here you can read, leaf, touch and browse the fascinating history of the two art forms.

For a premier dining experience, head over to the café inside the museum which offers outstanding art and design, in addition to an excellent view across the Ostre Anlaeg Park.

9. Tivoli

Opened in 1843, the Tivoli comprises the second oldest amusement park in the world, after the Dyrehavs Bakken Park. The most visited amusement park in Scandinavia, Tivoli is an experience ideal for any type of traveler.

The park is home to amusement park rides, romantic gardens, restaurants and a diversity of entertainment options. Visitors can simply enjoy the gardens or get some thrills by purchasing amusement park ride tickets separately.

The rides have all been designed to match the gardens and architecture of Tivoli. While some rides are wonderfully nostalgic, others match the expectations of the keenest thrill seekers. Adventure seekers can try the Vertigo, which turns riders upside down at 100km/h and was voted the Best Ride in Europe in 2014.

Tivoli also boasts one of the world's oldest wooden roller coasters known as Rutsjebanen, which was built in 1914. Other highlights among the many park attractions include the modern zero-G coaster, a flight stimulator and Himmelskibet, the tallest carousel in the world.

The massive Tivoli Concert Hall makes for another popular event location in the park. Other entertainment choices include the Pantomime Theater, as well as performances by Fredagsrock and the Tivoli Boys Guard, which take place every Friday in the summer. Some of events of the Copenhagen Jazz Festival concerts are also held at Tivoli.

With regards to food, Tivoli is equally diverse. A visit to the Tivoli gardens is definitely worth the vacation time of any food lover. While some Danes will bring a picnic, there really is a choice of everything available including traditional Danish cuisine to French bistro.

From late September to late October, the park is transformed for 'Halloween in Tivoli' events into an enchanted Halloween universe complete with witches, lanterns and pumpkins. This is followed by the beautiful and romantic Christmas market to mark 'Christmas in Tivoli' events which last until the end of the year.

Situated just a few minutes' walk from City Hall, close to Copenhagen Central Station, the gardens are today a national treasure. Fairy tale writer Hans Christian Andersen visited many times, as did Walt Disney who is said to have been inspired to create Disneyland following his visit to Tivoli. Many other celebrities have fallen in love with the gardens over the years.

The secret to Tivoli is the fact that it has something to offer everyone. Beautiful scenery with exotic architecture, lush gardens and historic buildings will greet the visitor who drops by. And at night, thousands of colored lights glow in the dark to create a very unique fairy tale atmosphere.

10. Nyhavn

The Nyhavn area of Copenhagen is typically Danish. Nyhavn or "New Harbour" was born in 1671 when King Christian V began its excavation as a way to develop the old capital city. For over 300 years since that period, the artificial canal of Nyhavn has been the site of pulsating life. Since inception, public houses, 'generous' women and merriment have always formed a part of Nyhavn's character.

Originally a busy commercial port where ships from all around the world would dock, Nyhavn was once packed with ale houses, pubs, sailors and ladies of pleasure. Today, its beautiful old houses have been renovated into classy restaurants that now dominate the old port. The location is now full of people enjoying the relaxed canal-side atmosphere, great food and music.

Over the years, many of the picturesque houses lining Nyhavn's quays have been home to prominent artists, poets and ballerinas. Danish author Hans Christian Andersen lived at no. 20, from which he wrote his fairy-tales: *The Princess and the Pea, The Tinder-Box*, as well as *Little Claus and Big Claus*. Arguably the most famous Dane, Andersen also lived in no. 67 for 20 years and in no. 18 for 2 years.

Another house - No. 9 is the oldest house in Nyhavn which dates from 1681. The house's design has not been altered since then.

Nyhavn is the ideal spot to end a long summer day. Have dinner at one of its cozy restaurants or do as the locals do and have some beers as you rest your feet at the quayside.

Nyhavn is also a popular starting point for canal boat tours. If you decide to go on one such tour, be sure to look out for *The Little Mermaid*, the diminutive bronze statue of the Hans Christian Andersen fairytale heroine and one of Copenhagen's most iconic landmarks since it was installed in 1913.

Printed in Great Britain
by Amazon